D0570053

British Columbian Salmon

A CELEBRATION OF PAINTINGS AND COOKERY

British Columbian Salmon

A Celebration of Paintings and Cookery

Compiled by Pamela McColl

Artwork by Bruce Muir

Foreword

David Griggs - (SEP) Department of Fisheries & Oceans
John Davis - Pacific Salmon Foundation

Introduced by Alan Haig-Brown

Terra Bella Publishers - Canada
West Vancouver, B.C.

Photographic Credits: Photo of man fishing courtesy of the Vancouver Public Library.
Photo of early settlers courtesy of The Salmon Village.

Edited by Brady Fotheringham
Typeset by Swee-Sim Tan
Designed by P.M. Art at Work Ltd.

Canadian Cataloguing in Publication Data
Main entry under title:
British Columbian Salmon

Includes index.
ISBN 1-896171-00-1 (BOUND). -- ISBN 1-896171-08-7 (PBK).

1. Cookery (Salmon) I. McColl, Pamela, 1958-
II. Muir, Bruce, 1953- III. Title.
TX748.S24B74 1994 641.6'92 C94-910392-6

Terra Bella Publishers - Canada
#10 - 2471 Marine Drive
West Vancouver, B.C. V7V 1L3
Phone/fax 604-926-2237

First Canadian Edition June 1994
Second Printing August 1994

Printed in Hong Kong by Kings Time Industries Ltd.

Special thanks to Peter Ng.

Terra Bella Publishers

In the 1850's the Hudson's Bay Company began exporting salt-cured B.C. salmon to a receptive world market. By the 1870's the first cannery was opened and a rapidly advancing fishing industry was well underway in B.C. In 1993 over 30 million salmon were caught by B.C. commercial fisheries, with 70% of the region's salmon products being exported to 34 countries. The salmon resource has made a considerable contribution to the economy and well-being of the province.

The story of B.C. salmon fishing has also been one of struggle. The building of the railroads, and the gold rush proved disruptive to the equilibrium of the rivers and streams, the essential lifeline of the salmon. Interference of the forestry and mining sectors and overfishing by the fishing industry itself brought salmon stock supplies into rapid decline.

Nature dealt a swift blow with a massive slide in 1914 at Hell's Gate in the Fraser River. The disruption caused was so severe that international headlines warned of the possible extinction of B.C. sockeye salmon.

The drastic decline of salmon stocks had a devastating effect on the fishing industry, jobs were lost and the economic consequences rippled through the fishing towns up and down the coast. By the 1970's there was widespread support for an action plan to reverse the decline and bring back the salmon to its historic levels.

In 1988 the Hell's Gate slide damage had been repaired, an initiative begun in the 1930's, and now salmon stocks are returning to acceptable levels. Natural disasters, diverse interests and economic motivations will continue to challenge the way of the salmon. The advantages to be found in the 1990's regarding preservation are: advanced scientific methodology, an ever-watchful world audience, and increased local involvement. The most important factor in salmon conservation today is the concerted effort to educate the young people of B.C. to be responsible, interactive and cooperative players in the on-going story of salmon.

This project on B.C. salmon cookery and the artwork of Bruce Muir began as an inspiration that would be both pleasing to the eye as well as the palate. When my research began I was aware of only a fraction of the effort currently going on in this province towards the enhancement and conservation of salmon. Tens of thousands of volunteers, extensive government and commercial initiatives and the vigilance of a host of non-profit organizations are to be applauded. This project has been eye opening to say the least and at times a humbling exercise. When the environment and salmon is concerned nothing should be taken for granted.

A list of recreation organizations appears at the end of this book.

A message from: Victor Elderton, Principal
North Vancouver Outdoor School, Brackendale, B.C.

The Squamish people speak of a guardian spirit which helps to remind us of our purpose.

Legend tells us that Wountie watches over our section of the Cheakamus River. This First Nations parable concerns a fisherman who caught all the salmon he needed for his family. As the salmon were so plentiful, he put his net back in the river to catch more. Wountie punished the greedy fisherman and several generations of his heirs by filling their nets with sticks instead of fish. Our modern civilization is confronted by similar circumstances. Misuse of natural resources makes news headlines daily. There is a growing demand for education concerned with wise land and resource use.

FOREWORD

David Griggs
Director, Salmonid Enhancement Program
Federal Department of Fisheries and Oceans

The salmon resource is of great importance to British Columbia. Historically it was the lifeblood of the indigenous peoples from the coast to the interior. With logging and trapping, it became an incentive for European colonization. In modern times it is the basis for a well-established commercial fishery serving both export and domestic markets, the salmon-farming industry and thriving sportfishing and tourism sectors. It continues to provide spiritual and economic sustenance to aboriginal communities province wide. Much of B.C.'s population, crowded into narrow settlements along the coast and river valleys, lives close to the salmon.

Unfortunately these same settlements, bringing with them rapid industrial and urban development, seriously threaten this magnificent natural legacy. Freshwater and ocean habitats have both been degraded by human activities which cause water shortages, nutrient and temperature imbalances, and pollution. Commercial fishing gear and vessels have become highly effective, freshwater and tidal recreational fishing is growing rapidly, and the aboriginal fishery has developed from food and ceremonial requirements to operations on a commercial scale. Combined, these factors have produced declines in the abundance of many salmon stocks even though restoration and enhancement efforts have provided an increased supply.

It is a primary responsibility of the Department of Fisheries and Oceans to conserve and protect Canadian fisheries resources.To that end, the federal/provincial Salmonid Enhancement Program (SEP) produces salmon in hatcheries and through other enhancement projects; the salmon are released to swim free and return for stock rebuilding.

Although SEP's large production facilities make an important contribution to the fisheries, I believe that in the long run environmentally based educational and community efforts will prove the most significant of our activities. I am therefore pleased to support this initiative, which seeks to broaden appreciation of the value of the salmon resource and ensure its stewardship for future generations of British Columbians.

John Davis
Executive Director
Pacific Salmon Foundation - Vancouver

We at the Pacific Salmon Foundation, a non-profit charitable organization, are dedicated to Pacific Salmon conservation, enhancement and restoration with a focus on education. There is no dispute that resource management mistakes have been made in the past and it is natural that they will be made in the future. Salmonid research has made tremendous strides over the past ten years. We continue to learn more about this amazing creature all the time. Biologists continue to make progress through researching habitat loss, new enhancement methods, predation, wild stock management and other conservation techniques.

The Pacific Salmon Foundation believes that educating young British Columbians about the importance and delicateness of our salmon resource will ensure the rebuilding of our stocks to historic levels in the years ahead.

It has been said that "we do not inherit from our ancestors as much as we borrow from our children." This is certainly true for Pacific Salmon.

I am very grateful to Bruce Muir for asking me to participate in this exciting new publication about B.C.'s most precious resource - salmon. The Foundation is currently supporting over sixty projects on a province wide basis generating support from over seven thousand volunteers.

The Flesh of the Sea Gods

An Introduction by Alan Haig-Brown

Growing up in Campbell River, as I did in the 1950's, salmon was a staple of our diet. Our household's primary source of income was my father's writing. Canadian writers then as now were not affluent. My Seattle bred mother, however, adapted well to the bountiful poverty of rural Vancouver Island. She grew a huge vegetable garden, made butter from our Jersey's thick cream and froze legs of lamb from our little farm for eating with her own mint jelly over the winter months. But in summer, like everyone else in town we ate salmon. I don't know where it all came from. I suppose my father caught some, although he preferred fishing the Campbell's summer steelhead which wasn't called salmon in those times but is now recognized as one of B.C.'s six salmon species. Most of our sea-caught salmon were donated by visiting tourists or family friends.

My frugal mother baked, stewed, pattied, sauced and wrung every last possible recipe out of these beautiful red fleshed fish. For me the greatest treat was always a salmon salad made with firm chunks of meat from the previous evening's baked dinner. Liberally mixed with fresh green peas and cubes of chilled cucumber and potato from mother's garden and nestled in crisp leaf lettuce it would be served in a large wooden salad bowl. Eaten in the shade of a big walnut tree with the Campbell River, passing at the bottom of the lawn where the salmon was most likely born, mother would announce with justifiable pride, "everything in the meal was grown on the place."

As a child most of the salmon I ate were sports caught, so they were most often the bright silver coho of eight or ten pounds. Occasionally there would be a larger spring with the colour of sea gold still shimmering down its sides. These were the fish that drew the world's anglers to our doorstep and the ones our neighbours lived on through the summer months.

Each species of salmon has distinct variations in flesh texture, oil content, colour and taste. Sports fishers flock to Campbell River to join the Tyee Club and qualify for achievement buttons by catching spring salmon over thirty pounds - Tyee they call them, chief among the salmon. To the commercial marketer of salmon, the species tend to be ranked according to their canning suitability and value on the world market. To the sports fisherman they are ranked by their size and fighting ferocity. The pride of the B.C. export market is the sockeye with its rich oil and colour.

At eighteen I joined the crew of a salmon seiner. My skipper was Herb Assu, grandson of Chief Billy Assu of the Cape Mudge Kwakiutl. Our cook was his wife Leoda, daughter of Francis Roberts who grew up to the north at Salmon River. Between them they carried the spirit of the First Nations people's special relation with salmon. Herb and Leoda showed me that all species of salmon, like all of one's children, are to be treasured each for their own unique qualities. Invariably the first set of the net that we made on the seine boat would catch a school of the lowest commercial and sport valued salmon, the pink salmon, often called the humpback for the shape of the male's back at spawning time.

Although there was obviously no need to voice the request, Herb would ask Leoda to make a pot of humpback stew for us to share at lunch to honour the new season and first salmon. A couple of firm bright three or four pound specimens would be chosen from the catch and taken into the galley. While the rest of us went on with fishing, Leoda once again proved the wisdom and beauty of simple cooking. When she called us to lunch in the little galley, the five of us had to enter according to our seating position in order to fit around the table where a big steaming pot of humpback stew rested. After the skipper had served himself, we each had a turn at digging the tasty morsels of pink meat and potato out of their cooking waters. Each ladleful brought with it a good number of fish eggs that Leoda had included in the stew. In a smaller bowl on the table was a beautifully clear and slightly yellow oil. Even the strong summer westerly blowing through the galley windows couldn't disperse the potent smell of the oil. This was eulachon oil, (gleetna), that over time I learned to garnish my stew with. Special food for special times.

Later in the summer the Fraser-bound sockeye arrived. The big runs of sockeye come in four year cycles, each named for the tributary of the Fraser in which they spawn. The Adams, Stewart, Quesnel and Chilco are among the largest of the runs. After reaching the mouth of the Fraser the Chilco River fish swim another five hundred miles through Hell's Gate and beyond to their spawning grounds in the midst of the Chilcotin plateau. Once in the river the ancient forces drive them on their urgent quest without eating again.

In their sea-time they have stored reserves of oil in their muscled bodies. When we caught them in Johnstone Straits, one hundred and fifty miles yet from the Fraser's mouth, they weighed several pounds. The canning companies paid top dollar for these wonderful fish and we sold most of our catch.

We kept some to can for our own winter food and on occasion, when the tide wasn't right to set the net, the cook would prepare one in the fashion familiar to most First Nations people. After cutting in from one side of the backbone she turned the fish and cut from the other side of the dorsal fin until the two cuts met at the belly, allowing the flesh to be taken from the fish in one piece like a chief's dance blanket. The opened blanket was placed in a lattice of cedar sticks. This in turn was clamped in larger pieces of untraditional but very effective one-inch dowels three feet long, purchased at the Campbell River Building Supply store and cut on the bandsaw two thirds in length.

Some of us from the crew would take two or three of these sticks with their carefully cut and mounted sockeye to the beach at a place called The Slide just below Harry Moon's Point. We built a driftwood fire and pushed the stakes into the beach gravel. As the heat of the fire worked its way into the dark red flesh, the leftover oil stored in the salmon began to boil. Some of it dripped to the hot gravel and evaporated, the aroma mingling back up with the meat above. As young crew members we turned the meat and debated whether it was best to cook the skin side or the cut side first. I can't remember if we ever proved either method to be more effective, but I do know that I have tried cooking salmon like this away from the beach and it never tasted as good.

Salmon is the food of our province and just as vintners have always been known for their wines, the subtleties of each variety are modified and enhanced by the location in which they are grown and the company in which they are consumed. Good lives have been spent sampling the familiar and searching for the extraordinary in both salmon and wine.

As one whose life has been so enriched I thank the salmon for giving the flesh of the sea gods to meals that I have eaten and for those that I will eat from recipes in this book.

A. H-B.

Art and Angling: The Paintings
B.C. Artist Bruce Muir

The paintings that appear in this book will be recognizable to many British Columbians as those of the much admired local artist Bruce Muir. As a painter of wildlife he has developed a strong following of enthusiasts for both his subject matter and his talent. Whether the viewer has seen his work on display at a fish and tackle shop, won a painting at a derby or bid on a favorite piece at an auction, the image be of fish or fowl, a Bruce Muir painting is admired for both its accuracy in detail and interpretive style.

In 1994 Bruce Muir won competitions that recognized him as the Artist of Year for both the B.C. Wildlife Federation and Trout Unlimited. In 1991 and 1992 the Canadian Government commemorated his Chinook Salmon paintings by producing stamps of his work for Sport Fishing Licenses.

Bruce Muir paintings are in the collections of R.J. Reynolds, Sonora Resort, Stubbs Island Charters, Pacific Salmon Foundation, First Group of Companies, Filler Drysdale, Trans Mountain Pipeline and the Trizec Corporation. Over the years Bruce Muir has given his works to be used in fund-raising efforts to the many recreational organizations he supports: chiefly the Vancouver Aquarium, Brant Festival, the Steelhead Society, Semiahmoo Hatchery, Richmond Nature Park and the Friends of Boundary Bay.

Bruce Muir was born in 1953 in Vancouver where he now resides.

"While painting is a satisfying career and a strong passion, I truly live to fish. The sight of a salmon taking a fly, lure or bait, is one I will never tire of. I gain inspiration for my art work while I am angling. A leaf floating through clear shallows, sunlight reflecting off a waterfall, or a black bear lounging on a fallen trunk; these images I cherish."

Bruce Muir

"A painter totally dedicated to his craft who skillfully combines his love for painting with his pursuit of fishing. A man who once told me that the reason he wished to have me as his representative was due to the fact that my gallery was close to the Capilano River."

David Edwards
Humberston Edwards Fine Art
West Vancouver, B.C.

Northern Steelhead

The Six Species of Pacific Westcoast Salmon

Chinook
Ivory to red in colour. Colour is not an indicator of taste; however, size is. The bigger the fish, the better the taste.

Also known as:
Tyee or King when over 30 pounds
Saumon royale - France
Königslachs - Germany
Masunosuke - Japan

Sockeye
Famous for its firm, red flesh. Sockeye's name is derived from the Native word for chief - Sau-kai.

Also known as:
Fraser and Thompson
Saumon rouge - France
Rotlachs - Germany
Benizake or benimasu - Japan

Chum
Pink to medium red flesh with a mild flavour.

Also known as:
Dog, Keta
Saumon kéta - France
Hundslachs - Germany
Sake, Shake - Japan

Pink
Delicate flavour and texture and light in colour.

Also known as:
Saumon rose - France
Buckellachs - Germany
Seppari masu - Japan

Coho
Red flesh, fine texture and full flavoured.

Also known as:
Silver
Saumon argenté - France
Silberlachs - Germany
Ginzake - Japan

The two sea-run trout:
Steelhead and Cutthroat
Legendary sports fishing species.

Also known as:
"the one that got away"

The Orford River

Salmon Cookery

Our household's culinary creed is a simple one. "If you can read you can cook." Logically of course this justifies a rather large collection of beautiful cookbooks. There is truth in this saying, however, and along with using only the freshest ingredients the best route to success in the kitchen is to arm yourself with a great repertoire of recipes. The rest is left to practice, a pinch of originality, presentation and the genuine pleasure you derive from cooking for others.

In this book you will find a selection of recipes that enhance the flavour of this king of all fish. Many of the recipes have come from coastal fishing lodges where preparing salmon for the table is a daily event. You will find cooking tips for a variety of cooking methods that will help you achieve great results. Some of the flavours are indigenous to B.C and others inspired by our multicultural culinary heritage.

I have fond memories of family and special occasions celebrated with a meal of well prepared B.C. salmon. It is my sincere hope that you will prepare all of the recipes in this book and that some of them will make their way into your family's treasury of tried and true recipes and that I have heightened your appetite for salmon.

Many thanks to those who have contributed the recipes.

Pamela McColl

The Canadian Cooking Theory

". . . the most important announcement in fish cookery of the century."

James Beard

Fresh fish is measured at its thickest point, its depth and not its width, and that it is cooked at exactly 10 minutes per inch (2.5 cm).

If the fish is in foil or paper add 5 minutes to the total. If it is frozen add 10 minutes per inch extra. Rolled or stuffed fish is to be measured after it is prepared. To time poached fish, wait until the poaching liquid has returned to the simmering point after the fish goes into the pot.

Selecting and Handling Salmon

When selecting a fresh salmon make sure the fish's eyes are clear and bright. The fish should not smell fishy and the skin should give slightly to the touch and then bounce back into shape.

To refrigerate fresh fish wipe it with a damp cloth and dry it with paper towels, double wrap it in foil and place it in a plastic bag. It keeps well for two days. If the fish is to be prepared the same day as purchased place the fish over a rack on a pan of ice. Cover the fish with a towel and surround with ice.

For freezing salmon wrap it in heavy foil and then place it in a plastic freezer bag. Date it prior to freezing it. Keeps up to 2 months.

The Various Cuts

Dressed - gills and entrails removed

Pan-dressed - head, tail, fins and scales removed

Steaks - cross cut slice with the salmon and centre bone in place

Fillets - pieces cut from the sides usually boneless without the skin

To remove the skin from a fish fillet use a flexible thin-bladed boning knife. Set the fish, skinside down, on a cutting surface with the thinner end closest to you. Cut close to the end down to the skin. Hold the skin and move the knife away from you along the skin. At the same time pulling on the skin. Remove bones with tweezers.

Chunks - larger pieces cut as steaks

Stamp River Falls

Cooking Tips

Individual recipe instructions may vary.

Steaming

Individual pieces are not to be too thick and should be in only one layer.
The fish needs to be at least one inch above the boiling water that itself needs to be kept at a vigorous boil. Have a kettle of water handy should additional boiling water be required to be added to the pan. Be sure the water is boiling prior to the fish being added. Cover the steamer tightly and be quick when checking if done.

Grilling

Always preheat and oil the grill rack before placing the fish on it. Do not crowd individual pieces of fish. The fish should be at room temperature before it is placed on the grill. Grill four inches from the hot heat.

Panfrying

Dry fish off prior to cooking. If the fish is to be floured do so right before cooking. The pan must be hot and well oiled but not smoking when you are ready to cook the fish.

Broiling

Always preheat the oven. Rub both sides of dry fish with oil and arrange without crowding on an oiled and preheated pan or rack.
You can also add variety to broiled fish by basting with melted butter, a splash of orange juice, extra marinate or even with a brushing of maple syrup. If you are broiling in a pan 1/8 inch of white wine or apple cider can be poured around the rim of the fish for interesting results.
Do not salt bare fish before broiling as it will possibly dry out the fish.

Baking

Lightly salt the interior of a whole dressed salmon if it is to be baked stuffed. Butter the outside and wrap it in foil. Cool the cooked salmon slightly before attempting to remove the wrap. If the fish is to be served cold leave it wrapped until it is needed. Baking will dry out a small piece of fish.

Poaching

Poached salmon's flavour improves if served the next day. Chilled cooked salmon needs to be allowed to briefly sit at room temperature prior to being served. A whole salmon needs approximately 30 minutes out of the refrigerator before being served.

To poach a whole salmon count on a salt water bath of 1 rounded tablespoon of salt to every 40 ounces of water. A splash of white wine vinegar or wrapping the fish in cheesecloth will help keep it intact.

Avoid poaching very thin fillets as the poaching process will take away from their flavour. Avoid poaching salmon steaks as the bone is unattractive and it is difficult to keep the ends intact. Use a classic court bouillon with care as one that is too spicy can distract from the flavour of the fish.

To poach the fish, cover it with the minimal amount of water. It helps to use a pan that just fits the fish. Bring the bath to a boil. When the fish is entered into the liquid be sure to keep it to a simmer and to never let the fish boil. Handle poached fish very carefully as it will be fragile from this cooking process. A slotted spatula works well in lifting the fish to a serving plate.

Microwaving

Arrange portions in a single layer and do not allow them to overlap. Test for doneness using great care in not overcooking with this method.

A Word About Wines and Salmon
from Robin Mines, restaurant critic and wine columnist

What wine do you serve with B.C. salmon? B.C. wine, naturally. From the familiar names of chardonnay and riesling to the delicious tongue-twisters of pinot auxerrois and ehrenfelser, there isn't a salmon recipe invented that won't find its perfect match in a wine with roots firmly planted in our province's grape-friendly soil.

British Columbians have had much to be proud of since the B.C. Wine Institute came up with a new set of wine standards in 1991; called Vintners Quality Alliance, the black and gold symbol on every bottle is your guarantee that the wine is 100% B.C.-grown and has passed a strict set of quality controls with flying colours.

The next logical question: which B.C. VQA wine with which B.C. salmon dish? Easy, you say. White wine with fish, red wine with meat, right? Wrong; that's an old relic of a rule, long overdue for the recycling box. Certainly, any of British Columbia's crisp, aromatic white wines are unbeatable in the company of salmon - just imagine a spicy, honey-scented gewurztraminer paired with the Salmon Papillotte with Ginger Parsley Butter, #17, or a smoky pinot gris with Continental B.C. Salmon, #20.

But B.C.'s red wines are equal to the task. Uniquely supple, they won't overwhelm the delicate taste and texture of salmon the way more aggressive contemporaries can. If you need convincing, tie on an apron, whip up a batch of Pan-fried Salmon with Cranberry Salsa, #10, and serve with an elegant, cranberry-red pinot noir from the Okanagan Valley - heaven. And if you plan to start your meal with a photogenic platter of Marinated Smoked Salmon, #2, or Sonora Resort's Gravlax, #4, a lively B.C. *methode champenoise* wine is the sparkling solution.

Whatever you do, when it comes to choosing a wine to complement your latest B.C. salmon creation, don't be intimidated. Whether you choose a white wine, a red wine, or a festive bottle of bubbly, if it's made in B.C., you're already home. Frankly, a fish never had it so good.

Double Header

RECIPE INDEX

1. The Only Barbecued Salmon
2. Marinated Smoked Salmon
3. West Coast Baked Salmon Fillet
4. Gravlax
5. Poached Salmon with Orange Thyme Mayonnaise
6. Salmon Wrapped in Phyllo Pastry with Tomato and Chive Coulis
7. Baked Salmon stuffed with Capers and Sweet Peppers
8. Poached Fillet of Salmonberry Beurre Blanc
9. Panfried Salmon Fillets with Huckleberry Confit
10. Panfried Salmon with Cranberry Salsa
11. Baked Salmon with grainy Mustard Lime Crust
12. Braised Salmon with Sweet Onions and Balsamic Vinegar
13. Salmon Steamed with Leek, Garlic and Lemongrass
14. Lodge Guests Favourite Pickled Salmon
15. Anytime of the Day Smoked Salmon
16. Poached Salmon in Champagne with B.C. Kiwi
17. Salmon Papillote (parcels) with Ginger Parsley Butter
18. Broiled Rosemary Needles Salmon Fillets
19. Mayonnaise Salmon
20. Continental B.C. Salmon
21. Marinated Westcoast Salmon Fillet
22. Cedar Plank Salmon with Okanagan Apples

Special thanks to the following contributors:

(1-3) David Veljacic - 1991 Canadian Barbecue Champion; (4-13) Wayne Sjothun - Sonora Resort, Campbell River; (14) Pat Ardley, River's Lodge, Rivers Inlet; (19) Bill Otway, Recreational Fisheries Coordinator, Ombudsman, Pacific Region, DFO, Canadian Outdoorsman of the Year 1982; (20) Dale McGee - Peregrine Lodge, Queen Charlotte Islands; (21) Lars Jorgensen, Hakai Beach Resort

RECIPES

#1

The Only Barbecued Salmon

1 3-4 pound salmon fillet (deboned)
10 large garlic cloves
4 tablespoons finely chopped parsley
1 1/2 tablespoons finely minced sun dried tomatoes
1/4 cup olive oil
1 teaspoon salt

With the flat of a wide bladed knife crush the garlic cloves, chop them up, pour the salt over the cloves and grind them with the flat of the knife. Combine the garlic, parsley, sun dried tomatoes and olive oil in a covered jar and allow to sit overnight in your fridge. With a very sharp knife, cut two lengthwise slits in the salmon fillet, dividing the surface of the fish into thirds. Cut to the skin, but not going through it.

Spread half the garlic mixture over the salmon fillet and into the slits, place on the grill in a gas barbecue at "low" temperature and close the lid. Cook for 15 minutes. Spread remaining garlic mixture on the salmon fillet, close the lid and turn the temperature to "medium" and cook for another 15 minutes, or test the salmon to see if it is done.

Remove salmon from the grill by inserting spatulas between the skin and the flesh of the salmon fillet, lifting the flesh, but leaving the skin on the grill. Place the skinless and boneless salmon fillet on a bed of fresh green lettuce.

#2

Marinated Smoked Salmon

2 pounds smoked salmon (cold smoked lox)
2 large finely shredded onions
1 tablespoon black pepper
1 cup olive oil
1/4 cup white vinegar
1/8 cup balsamic vinegar
Iceberg lettuce shredded

Slice the salmon 1/8 inch slices.

In a glass food container place a thin layer of onion, followed with a layer of salmon, sprinkle with black pepper. Continue this until the salmon is used up, finishing off with onion. Pour the olive oil mixture over this so it is covered with the liquid. Seal the container and place in the refrigerator for 1-2 days. During this time you should turn the container upside down several times.

With a pair of tongs place 3-4 slices of salmon and onion on some shredded lettuce. Serve with sliced Baguette Bread. This can stay refrigerated for 2-3 weeks.

#3

West Coast Baked Salmon Fillet

2 2 - 3 pound salmon fillets (deboned)
3 large leeks finely minced
1 large chopped white onion
1 small chopped celery heart
6 large minced garlic cloves
8 ounces tomato sauce
1 litre V8 juice
1/2 cup olive oil
Black pepper
1 tablespoon oregano
Salt to taste

Pour half the olive oil in a Pyrex dish then place the fillets in the dish. Sprinkle well with the black pepper and bake in the oven at 375 degrees until done, approximately 20 minutes. Remove from the oven, drain off all the oil and set aside. In a heavy bottomed stainless steel pot use the remaining olive oil to sauté the leeks, onion, celery hearts and garlic, until very limp. Add the oregano, tomato sauce and half of the V8 juice, simmer for 1/2 hour. If the sauce is too thick add a little more V8 juice. Pour this over the salmon and bake in the oven at 400 degrees until the sauce begins to bubble around the fillets.

#4

Gravlax

2 sides salmon skin on (deboned)
2 cups fresh dill
5 ounces coarse salt
3 ounces sugar
3 tablespoons lemon juice
1 tablespoon crushed white peppercorns
4 ounces Aquavit
2 tablespoons mustard seed

Lay fillets skin down in a shallow dish. Combine all ingredients except dill in a bowl. Rub each fillet with mixture, then sprinkle chopped dill evenly across each fillet. Cover fillets with plastic film, and place weighted object to press down fish. Place in the refrigerator, turning once a day for 3 days. After third day remove fillets, pour off excess liquid, and slice fish on the diagonal into thin slices and serve with mustard sauce.

Mustard sauce

1 egg
1 cup vegetable oil
1/4 cup olive oil
1 tablespoon lemon juice
1 tablespoon white wine
4 tablespoons Dijon mustard
Salt and pepper to taste

Blend egg in a food processor adding oil slowly in a stream. Add lemon, wine and mustard, season with salt and pepper.

#5

Poached Salmon with Orange Thyme Mayonnaise

Court Bouillon
6 cups fish stock
1/2 cup white wine
1 medium onion peeled
2 celery stalks
1 juiced lemon
1 tablespoon peppercorns
1 bay leaf
2 sprigs of fresh herbs

Simmer all for 10 minutes and strain out the spices and herbs. Place fish in simmering stock and poach for 5-8 minutes depending on the thickness.

Mayonnaise

1/4 cup minced onion
1/4 cup white wine
1 free range egg
1 egg yolk
1 cup vegetable oil
1/4 cup olive oil
Juice and zest of 1 orange
1 tablespoon fresh thyme leaves
Salt and pepper

Sauté the onion until it is transparent. Add the wine, juice and zest of orange and the thyme. Reduce over heat until it equals 2 tablespoons. Blend egg in a food processor adding the oil in a slow and steady stream until the mixture emulsifies. Mix with the reduced liquid and season. Refrigerate for two hours before serving.

#6

Salmon Wrapped in Phyllo Pastry with Tomato and Chive Coulis

4 4 ounce salmon fillets
8 sheets phyllo pastry (preferably fresh)
4 tablespoons clarified unsalted butter
3 tablespoons minced shallots
1 tablespoon olive oil
1 cup tomato concassé (peeled, seeded, diced)

Brush phyllo sheets with the clarified butter. Place two sheets on top of one another for each of the salmon portions. Place seasoned salmon on the phyllo and fold over the pastry to form an envelope. Brush the top of the pastry parcel with the butter. Place on a baking sheet and bake in a preheated oven at 350 degrees. Cooking time is determined by the thickness of the fillets. Pastry will be a golden brown.

Sauce

Sauté shallots in the olive oil until soft, add tomatoes and simmer for 10 minutes. Pureé this mixture in a food processor until smooth. Add chives just before serving. Serve salmon parcels onto the sauce.

7

Baked Salmon stuffed with Capers and Sweet Peppers

1 5-8 pound whole salmon bones removed
4 tablespoons butter
3 cups fresh bread with crusts removed and cubed
1/2 cup diced onion
1/2 cup diced celery
1/4 cup capers
1/2 cup red pepper
2 tablespoons chopped fresh herbs
fish stock to moisten
salt and pepper to taste

Sauté the onion, celery and peppers in the butter until soft. Add capers, herbs and the bread cubes stirring well. Add the fish stock just to moisten. Season and let cool. Place a one inch layer of stuffing in the fish and double wrap the fish in foil. On a baking sheet cook the fish at 10 minutes per 1 inch 375 degree oven.

#8

Poached Fillet of Salmonberry Beurre Blanc

4 4 ounce salmon fillets
1 cup salmonberries (optional - blueberries)
1 tablespoon chopped shallots
8 ounces butter
4 ounces white wine
Salt and pepper to taste
1 teaspoon lemon juice

Poaching salmon as in recipe for Poached Salmon with Orange Thyme Mayonnaise. Sauté shallots in 1 teaspoon butter until transparent. Add berries and the white wine and reduce until liquid is reduced to 2 tablespoons (approximately). Let cool slightly, add room temperature butter stirring in 1 tablespoon at a time until it is fully incorporated. Season with salt, pepper and lemon juice.

#9

Panfried Salmon Fillets with Huckleberry Confit

4 6 ounce skinned and deboned fillets
1/2 cup red huckleberries
1/2 cup black huckleberries
2 tablespoons sugar
2 tablespoons raspberry wine vinegar
1/2 teaspoon lemon zest
Salt and pepper to taste

In a hot skillet, coated lightly with vegetable oil, sear the fillet until golden brown, turn, lower the heat slightly and finish cooking.

Sauce

Caramelize sugar in a thick bottomed saucepan, add vinegar and stir until the sugar is dissolved completely. Add the berries, zest, salt and pepper cooking for 2 minutes. Serve over the prepared cooked salmon.

#10

Panfried Salmon with Cranberry Salsa

4 4 ounce salmon fillets
1 cup fresh or frozen cranberries coarsely chopped
1/4 cup red onion finely diced
1/4 cup green pepper finely diced
2 tablespoons raspberry vinegar
2 tablespoons sugar
1 tablespoon chopped parsley
1 tablespoon lemon zest finely chopped
1 small jalepeno chopped
3 tablespoons olive oil
Salt and pepper to taste

Salsa

Combine all the ingredients and cover. Let sit for 3 hours prior to serving. Serve under or to the side of the salmon.

In a sauté pan or skillet that has been lightly coated with vegetable oil panfry the fish over medium high heat. Turn once.

Fat free alternate method: use non-stick cooking paper.

#11

Baked Salmon with grainy Mustard Lime Crust

8-12 ounces salmon fillet cut into portions
6 tablespoons grainy mustard
Juice and zest of 1 lime

Chop zest very fine and mix with the juice and the mustard. Coat each portion of salmon with the mustard mixture, place on an oiled baking sheet and bake in a 375 degree oven with the time determined by the size of the fillets.

#12

Braised Salmon with Sweet Onions and Balsamic Vinegar

4 4 ounce boneless salmon fillets or steaks
3 c. sliced sweet onions (maui or walla walla)
1 tablespoon olive oil
1/2 teaspoon chopped garlic
3 tablespoons balsamic vinegar
Salt and pepper to taste

Sauté the onion and the garlic in the olive oil until they are soft and transparent. Place onions in a ceramic baking dish, place the salmon on the onions and sprinkle with salt and pepper and then the vinegar. Cover the dish with foil and bake at 350 degrees for 10-12 minutes.

Salmon Steamed with Leek, Garlic and Lemongrass

4 4 ounce salmon steaks
2 tablespoons julienned leeks
1 tablespoon minced garlic
1 stalk lemon grass cut into 1 inch pieces
(lemon peel can be substituted)
2 tablespoons light soy
1 tablespoon mirin (sweetened rice wine)
1 tablespoon rice vinegar
Pepper to taste

Place salmon steaks on a serving plate. Prepare a Chinese bamboo steamer with water. Put the lemon grass into the water. Sprinkle salmon with the garlic and the leeks. Steam fish for 4-6 minutes. Remove the fish. Prepare a sauce with the light soy, mirin, vinegar and pepper.

#14

Lodge Guests Favourite Pickled Salmon

Make a solution of the following ingredients and boil for 10 minutes.

2 cups vinegar
3/4 cup water
2 tablespoons honey
2 tablespoons coarse salt
3 tablespoons peppercorns
(or a combination of peppercorns and whole allspice)

Put pieces of salmon in the solution and simmer for 3-5 minutes or until just cooked. Place salmon in a glass dish and cover with the pickling liquid. Put slices of Spanish onion in the liquid and keep refrigerated up to three weeks. Serve with assorted breads and sliced onions. Drizzle brine over individual servings.

#15

Anytime of the Day Smoked Salmon

4 free range eggs
2 tablespoons whole milk
1 teaspoon butter
2 tablespoons smoked salmon diced

Break the eggs and add the milk and seasonings. Whisk until well mixed. Put the butter in a cold saucepan and melt on low and pour in the eggs and stir until scrambled. Just before the eggs are done add the salmon. Stir gently.

#16

Poached Salmon with Champagne with B.C. Kiwi

4 4 ounce salmon fillets
2 cups champagne
2 cups whipping cream
2 tablespoons unsalted butter
3 kiwi peeled and sliced

Boil champagne until it is reduced by half. Remove from heat and add cream. Return to a simmer and add salmon for 5 minutes. Place fan of kiwi on the fish in the pan and cook 3 minutes more. Remove salmon and keep warm. Add the butter to the sauce and reduce to approximately 1 cup. Pour over salmon.

#17

Salmon Papillote (parcels) with Ginger Parsley Butter

4 ounce fillet per portion
1/2 ounce butter per portion
1 teaspoon finely chopped parsley (cilantro can be substituted)
1 teaspoon finely grated ginger

Salt the fish lightly on both sides. Let stand for ten minutes. Cream the butter with the ginger and add the parsley. Smear a little of the creamed butter mixture on a sheet of greaseproof paper or tin foil. Place the salmon portion on the sheet, spread the remaining portion of the butter mixture on top of the fish. Fold over the parcel and seal the edges. Bake in a preheated 350 degree oven and bake for 10-12 minutes.

#18

Broiled Rosemary Needles Salmon Fillets

4 4 ounce salmon fillets
2 tablespoons olive oil
Juice and zest of 1 lemon
1 tablespoon rosemary needles dried and crumbled
1/4 cup white wine
2 tablespoons clarified butter

Pat fillets dry with paper towel. Brush both sides with olive oil. Place fillets in a shallow oven pan. Pour wine around the fish. Place under hot broiler for 1 minute. Baste with a mixture of the remaining olive oil, butter, rosemary and lemon. Broil 5 minutes more without turning.

#19

Mayonnaise Salmon

6-8 pound salmon fillet
Fresh ginger or 1 teaspoon powdered ginger
Mayonnaise (See recipe #5)
Brown sugar
Salt and pepper to taste

Line a shallow roasting pan with foil. Brush lightly with oil and place the fillet skin side down in the pan. Salt and pepper to taste. Grate a fine sprinkling of fresh ginger over the fish. Spread a thin layer of mayonnaise over the top of the fillet covering the exposed area completely. The ginger can be added to the mayonnaise to ease the preparation, although the ginger will not have the same impact on the fish. Sprinkle the brown sugar over the top. Place in a 350 degree preheated oven and bake (25-30 minutes for a 6-8 pound fillet.) For a very large fillet the oven should be turned down for the last 5 minutes to 325 degrees.

#20

Continental B.C. Salmon

1/4 lb. melted butter
1/4 cup finely chopped shallots
1/2 pound sliced mushrooms
10 individual portions of salmon fillets
1/2 pound ground salmon (seasoned with salt, pepper and lemon juice)
10 large raw oysters
20 shelled precooked shrimps
1/4 cup white wine
3 cups half and half cream
1 tablespoon cornstarch
1/4 teaspoon cayenne pepper

Pour melted butter into a shallow saucepan, add the shallots and mushrooms. Arrange the fillets over the vegetables.

Spread the raw ground salmon mixture over the fillets and top each portion with an oyster and two shrimp on either side of the oysters. Cover the pan and cook over a medium heat and simmer for ten minutes. Uncover and add the white wine. Cover and cook for 15 minutes. Remove fish from the pan to a preheated serving platter. Blend the cornstarch with the cayenne into the cream, add to the juices in the pan, and bring to a fast boil, stirring constantly. Season with salt and pepper.

Pour over the fish and serve.

#21

Marinated Westcoast Salmon Fillet

2 pound salmon fillet, skin on
2 1/2 ounces brown sugar
1 teaspoon juniper berries, crushed
1 1/2 ounces coarse salt
1 teaspoon crushed black pepper
1/4 bunch fresh dill, chopped
3/4 ounce gin

Marinate: Place salmon in a flat ovenproof dish, skin side down. Mix remainder of ingredients in a small bowl and spread evenly over salmon. Let sit in fridge for 4 hours minimum. Remove salmon from fridge one hour before cooking and pour off juices and reserve for sauce.

To cook salmon, preheat oven to 400 degrees and bake for 15 to 20 minutes maximum.

Sauce

1 ounce brown sugar
2 ounces dijon mustard
1/4 bunch fresh dill, chopped
2 1/4 ounces vegetable oil
1/2 lemon, juice only
tabasco to taste
5 tablespoons whipped whipping cream
1 tablespoon juice from marinade

Mix brown sugar and dijon mustard in a bowl and slowly whip in the vegetable oil. Add remaining ingredients, and at the end fold in whipped cream.

Serving suggestion: Divide baked salmon into four or five portions and serve with grilled spring vegetables. Top salmon with sauce at the last minute.

#22

Cedar Plank Salmon with Okanagan Apples

2 pound salmon fillet
untreated cedar plank
3 McIntosh apples cut into 1/4 inch slices
1 cup fresh apple juice or cider
1/4 cup fino sherry
3 tablespoons unsalted butter
1 tablespoon walnut oil

Marinate the salmon in the apple juice and sherry for two hours.

Prepare the cedar plank by submerging it in cold water for two hours. Remove the plank and place in a 450 degree oven for ten minutes. Place the salmon on the plank, return to the oven and cook at 10 minutes per inch.

Melt the butter and walnut oil in a sauté pan and cook the apples until soft. Remove the apples and keep warm. Deglaze the pan with the marinate and reduce by half.

Place salmon portions on warmed plates with a serving of the apples on the side. Drizzle two tablespoons of the sauce over the salmon.

Recreational Organizations of Special Mention

B.C. Wildlife Federation. The B.C.W.F.'s 40,000 membership is comprised primarily of the various fish and game clubs located in almost every community in the province. The Wildlife Federation has a long history of commitment to the fishery resource and has maintained an active and effective lobby on its behalf. They also sponsor a Wilderness Watch programme which helps police fish and wildlife laws. Langley 604-533-2293

The Steelhead Society of B.C. As a conservation organization the primary function of the Society at its inception was to act as an informed voice on behalf of the steelhead salmon. The organization has expanded its concern to include other salmon species, trout and aquatic environment. P.O. Box 33947 Station D Vancouver V6J 4L7

British Columbia Conservation Foundation was formed in 1967 by the B.C. Wildlife Federation to raise and hold funds for various conservation programmes around the province. Since 1986 the Foundation has supervised the expenditure of fifteen million dollars and facilitated over 665 conservation projects. Surrey 604-576-1433

The Nature Trust of B.C. is responsible for the purchase and preservation of the property at the Roderick Haig Brown Reserve on the Adams River which preserves the habitat of the world famous Adams River Sockeye Run. 604-925-1128

Pacific Salmon Foundation. Their major objective is the enhancement and preservation of Pacific salmon and promoting the conservation ethic through education. The Foundation's volunteer Board of Directors is comprised of twenty members representing the Native, Commercial and Recreational fishing sectors. The Foundation is currently supporting over sixty projects generating support from over seven thousand volunteers. Vancouver 604-669-3710